I0122659

An Array of Vapour

Peter Lilly

TSL Publications

First published in Great Britain in 2024
By TSL Publications, Rickmansworth

Copyright © 2024 Peter Lilly

ISBN: 978-1-915660-74-9

Cover by
Silje Lilly

Contents

Dedication and Thanks

These poems are dedicated to the memory of Andrew Erskine, the workers and service users of New Hope homelessness charity in Watford, England, and to all those who are forced to make a home wherever they can.

Firstly, I would like to thank my wonderful wife Silje, for her endless love, encouragement and support, and whose own works of creativity and compassion never cease to inspire and amaze me. Thanks to her also for the wonderful cover design and artwork. Thanks to our beautiful son for being so full of life and joy, and to my family, and family-in-law for encouraging me in my writing over many years. I want to thank Anne Samson and TSL for publishing this book, and for the wonderful way they partner with their authors. A special thanks to my friends and poets who helped with feedback and writing the blurbs: To Malcolm Guite for being a unique and endless source of inspiration and encouragement. To Alastair McIntosh for his inspiring work with place and people, and for helping me finish the poem that was inspired by his work. To Deryck Robertson for his service to the poetry community through the amazing Paddler Press Journal. To Matthew Heasman for the inspiring work he continues to do as CEO of the Watford charity New Hope. I would also like to thank all of my colleagues who worked at New Hope between 2010 and 2015, for your beautiful hearts and loving hard work. Thank you also to all the service users, your honesty, humour, determination, vulnerability and beautiful humanity shaped these poems, and continue to shape me.

Acknowledgments

Thanks to the following publications for previously publishing some of these poems: *Archetype Journal, Across the Margin, Barehands Poetry, Beyond Words Literary Magazine, Dreich Magazine, Dreich Broad, Green Ink Poetry, Heart of Flesh Literary Journal, Lothlorien Poetry Journal, The Minison Project, Radix Magazine,* the 2018 Anthology *'Please Hear What I'm Not Saying'* by *Fly on the Wall Press,* and the *Dead Letter Radio Podcast.* Thanks to the editors of these publications for sharing, and for your input in shaping, many of the poems in this book.

An Array of Vapour

Too often ending with a choice
that betrays the desperation.
Vapour disperses to become air,
as briefly perceived as the echoes of their eulogy.

Many find the courage to continue
in synthesised prescriptions that silence and sedate,
for there is now nothing but the ends of tethers
for those who care for a living.

Yet, people are collateral damage
of the repeated attempts
to rebuild Babel's tower on our soil.
They see the spire piercing hell,
and are sectioned.

The sufferers become the scapegoats.
Frozen in the system's lens,
and in the winter's cold.

Yet despite the script
recovery can germinate.

Crystalised vapour can proudly exhibit
the humble kintsugi beauty
of anterior struggle.

Violent Sleep...

*Too often ending with a choice
that betrays the desperation.
Vapour disperses to become air
as briefly perceived, as the echoes of their eulogy...*

Eyes

That night you persistently asked
leading questions about nothing,
they were leading downwards.
And there I was, trying
to phrase an elusive answer,
while you were trying
to find a reason to breathe.

The next morning, you had two pairs of eyes.
One, attempting to look so determined,
glinting as they darted up and down the corridor,
like something untamed meeting unnatural torch-light.
You told me I needed to call the police,
that this time they needed to take you away.
The other pair was static, and unmistakably dead.

Nine-nine-nine,
we dialed a third time in eight hours.
Colour slowly drained from your face
as we started the compressions.
I felt your rib-cage crack
as we fought for breath you did not want.

I checked your throat for blockages,
noticing your missing teeth,
remembering your last hot meal,
the charity of a well-meaning bystander,
who promptly moved on.
I can still see your motionless tongue.
And those eyes, already gone.

Choices

Time was stretched by your death.
Often you'd crack your bones
and talk about boats.

Your entire life was caught
between lethargic contentment
and daydream ambition.

One is carbon monoxide,
the other is ceasing to breathe.

Time was stretched by your death
as you labelled thin skin
with wind-swept purpose. Still
talking about boats.

Rough

If only the ground was soft and warm,
and morning's light greeted me
with a dew of feathery comfort.

A slumber enforced sobriety beats
a hangover through my skull.

If only the rain would retain
the nonchalance of intoxication,
and the falling leaves were sterling.

A staccato crescendo of approaching feet
demands I rise or hide.

If only they could see me,
collect me, transport me, and
like discarded cardboard, transform me.

It Stoppeth One of Three

Pain dictates like inclement weather
winter taunts every lack.

Your pain is my albatross,
my boat full of the damned,
bringing perspective,
breaking proportion,
slicing its mirrors into time.
Your pain is the ancient madman
calling me from the damnation
of my own consideration,
the hell of numbness and safety,
into the real, fortuitous
and ever testing volatility
of living.

This poem contains several deliberate allusions to the epic poem 'The Rime of the
Ancient Mariner' by Samuel Taylor Coleridge.

Agony

Agony doesn't talk, it shivers.
It tries to blink away expression
in wallpaper clichés.
It is the bloodshot eyes beneath.

Agony maligns teeth in tension.
It thinks in spirals of acute intentions
in the deliberate delirium
of endless cause and effect.

To Androcles

Death is not a greenhouse, full of CO_2
Feeding the season's tomatoes.

It is devoid of green things
And the exchange of poisons.

I'm too young to dwell on death's estate,
Feeding on its empty plates.

But I feel it, mostly in dearth,
Particularly of the motivation to move.

It grows in my paw
Like a malignant thorn.

Violent Sleep

You drink deeply from the methadone bottle.
The prescription suicide juice
begins peacefully shutting you down.
But there is still something violent
in a death like this.

Despite the fact that it is sleep
your dreaming heart merely forgets to beat,
your drowsy lungs drift on
with faint crackles that eventually become
silence and stillness.
There is still something violent in this sleep.

Empty capillaries pale the skin,
and your face becomes
merely pencil drawn features on grey-white paper.
Red splashes from your nose,
yellow dribbles from your mouth,
as you bleed and vomit Pollock-like masterpiece
onto your sketch face.
You are a static work of tragic art.
The expressionism of empty rest.

And there is something violent here.
It is numb asphyxiation.
It is anaesthetised infarction.
It is the empty space in your infant's growth,
which is the greatest loss of the broken legacy
of your choice of a violent sleep
that you could not feel.

Faulty Medicine...

... Many find the courage to continue
in synthesised prescriptions that silence and sedate,
for there is now nothing but the ends of tethers
for those who care for a living...

Christmas Hit

There's a clamour in your veins
hoping for some warmth.

Crisp futures thaw slowly
and collage the pavement
with decaying autumn.

There's a clamour in your veins
and your blood is sedated.

The frost-bite doesn't bother you
when you're nodding through festive freeze,
unaware of your own shivering.

There's a clamour in your veins
soothing you from conscious fears.

Childhood promises are all cooked up from poppies,
and when you're permeated with gear
it feels like Christmas.

There's a clamour in your veins;
track-marks leading from pinpricks to amputation.

The pain of withdrawal could bring the beauty of future,
but you're perforated by these fairy lights
that suck significance from nature.

Questions for a Wreck

The brand-new paving of this town is cracking,
conforming to your abscessed feet.
Your veins have all given up carrying life
against that tidal poison you inject.
Your swollen fingers are forever cold,
premature of your death.

And   I have these intrusive questions
yet   I have not the right to ask,
only wonder, sponging your lesions
As the warm basin turns pink.

How can you know
which wounds to patch up first
so the momentum of healing
can carry you through detox
to independence?

How many labels of fame
can you self-proclaim
As you cram a thousand vocations
into your clouded pupils?

How many breeds of broken
can you scar onto flesh,
as you try to understand the seeds?

True, they must die to give birth to life,
but sometimes death
is simply,
death.

How many shades of beauty
will you have to acknowledge
for hope to set and dry over these fissures
so your path can bear the weight
of your shivering future?

Flame, Spoon, Needle, Numb.

Golden conversations roll across the ocean's surface
but there is a good reason for this.
I was in the vomit of liquid laughter
where white lines are chased by a black horse.
Inside a fiction of a clean addiction and routine.
Yet, there's good reason for this.

Twisted chariots came to take me away this morning,
but I didn't want to leave with them
because they did not know my name,
and I'm in no mood to make new friends.

This is all I need:
Flame.
Spoon.
Needle.
Numb.
This is my temporary alleviation
through which I'm sooner to expire.
I'll make my bed of soft light
that slowly soothes the skin
To transmute into broken bottles,
and the piss stain that warms
And grows cold.
I'm sure time does still move
before I soften the asphalt
With the sweat of withdrawal.
But this is me, alone.
When *my* time stands still.

Measuring With Money

There is a crooked ruler
measuring the growing mould of success
which eats masterpiece pages.

It inspires fathers
to chase their infants into the asphalt,
to pass on the splintered baton
of generational responsibility.

Children's bite wounds push them
to sharpen their own teeth,
and motivate their own kin to let go,
repeat, and fall into hepatitis spikes,
themselves becoming absent fathers.

This relay of abuse,
is the perpetual motion
of bottomless sinking.

Unmedicated

I need these questions
to douse my rage.

I keep trying
to clean my heart
with filthy hands.

I've been gritting my teeth together,
wanting to grind my skull into white powder
and wash my exposed memories
into liquid ambience.

I dream of her every night.
I swallow that dream each morning.
Every day it sticks in my throat.

The essence of her agony
still haunts me now.

Red

Listen.

Your bellowing lungs
were caged by
the folding of years,
trapping space in time.
You were merely left observing.

Silent individual,

A savage of your self-made habitat,
listing your ever absent dreams
and forever drowning
in the distractions
of diluted blood.

Pink poisons:

A candy trail
that sighs out life
in mere moments
of induced palpitations.
But you can breathe.

Diluted pink poisons:

A candy trail that sighs out life
is enough to be ignored.
There is a better way to grow
than trying to climb
those momentary lightning bolts.

They dull your imagination,

Slicing a burning wound in the sky,
singeing your eye.
The illuminated road
was but a misdirection.
There's a better way to grow.

Ascend above dread and negation.

Climb into the blackness.
Break the tinted window of the night
to let ebony infect this twisting globe
with an innocence that does not deny
the redness of blood.

A Man Without a Mirror

He stood there
with all the bored self-assurance
of a part-time life-model,
disinterested in the
impressions and expressions
of the scrutiny of his form.

With the apathetic vulnerability
of glazed eyes above
pale skin folds, below
unflattering lighting, before
focused pupils.

And there was something beautiful
in his anti-catwalk confidence,
the antonym of every script
of social media cameras
that keep the rest of us
glancing at mirrors.

Grace

Crumbs of grace fall,
bounce off your shoes
and surround your feet
in constellations of disregard.

But do not despair!
though they are precious pieces
they are but fragments of the costliest treasure,
spread above, waiting for you to jump
and be submerged.

A Vision of Life

You told me of the light
that gets bigger as you step towards it.
How it stretches out your shadow
to darken the entirety of your infancy.
That, when curiosity grabs you,
and you turn to view your past,
all the diversity of your previous life
is indistinguishably dark   and lifeless.

You told me that one day you will stand inside the light.
That no matter where you turn all will be shadowless.
Even those years you need to forget,
will be drowned in the effervescence.
Deep inside the night of your pupils
I could see its glimmer   growing.

Vaporous Walls...

*... Yet, people are collateral damage
of the repeated attempts
to rebuild Babel's tower, on our soil.
They see the spire piercing hell,
And are sectioned...*

Discharged

Where was my medicine?

Lost in the folds of my
ligature accessory.

My instrument of
fashionable self-harm.
It was a beautiful scarf

until I made it my medicine.

Where was my medicine?

Under the skin
of my forearms.

I tried to release it,
but beneath the surface
it is red liquid, and so complex.

I couldn't find my medicine,

so, they discharged me
from their care.

Now, I can persevere,
Sorting through blades and nooses
in hope that I find my medicine.

Becoming Paper

Sometimes I feel I'm becoming paper
Squeezing myself into the pre-written.
My paragraph days are nonsensical
Like strings of beach-junk pearls: recycled
Discards; mismatched beauty; value stricken.
I feel my pages dampen in the vapour
Of where I have been left to wither, like
Would-be-dictators in institutions.
The pages you wanted photocopied?
Crease those moments upon themselves. I'll strike
A match and let fire be my ablution,
For it is the truth, in heat, embodied.
You can keep your paper, recounting my death.
I'll write my own eulogy, but with breath.

Terrifying Best Intentions

You wanted to be social bleach
that could turn the clandestine candescent.
      Class-cleansing, normalising
       the contours of the brain.
Cloud of thought, electrical storm,
           synapses born.

But a difference is not an ailment.

Exit Grief

Winter night cold waits
frosting the grass with delicate
threats of treacherous beauty,
where breath-mist from an inert body
is the only proof of life.

Foxes scamper where sight meets shadow.
Litter is discarded chaos theory
arguing with landfills and origami,
but the pattern is gravity.

The road is the noblest of choices.

A wide window reveals the hoards,
their uniform silhouettes
are attempts to disguise varied faces.
Collective consciousness is an idiot.

The road is the noblest choice.

Skin

Skin chases skin alone,
stretching itself until
it dulls every window,
pouring restlessness into home.

Skin knows its pores are suffocating,
drawing its own ink
to display fading ideas as permanent,
tracing these tattoos, hallucinating.

Skin licks mirror's cold
and clouds wet circles,

yet at its most lucid
it realises its own
translucence.

Breathe

Grapple	here	
in	vines	
where	dampness	
is	breath,	
and	crystal	futures
paint	cold	metaphors
onto	leaking	minds.

The	constant	
dull	drip	
vacates	to	
memories	or	
make	believe,	both
elsewhere,	and	without
the	dynamism	of

                    breath.

A Night on The Street

Condensation breath
and cold concrete.
I'll breathe a heavy dew
onto this street.

Trees are but a partial shelter,
a dilapidated house.
My breath is enough to water
and feed them with growth.

I'm glad the shelters
are full.

There are new scars this morning
all on the soles of my feet.
Hazy steps, shrouded in dream,
leave discomfort for the walking.

There are new scars this morning,
and the world has learnt to hate
the marks of beautiful healing
blemishing me.

Drizzle

Wattled days, damp and dense,
hang from the mildewed wall of time
like wet wallpaper. So full
of what would be thirsted for
if it wasn't for the constant drizzle.

There is a loneliness you
can only feel when your socks are soaked.
Cold and throaty, it makes sure
you know your place, and that your place
is not habitable.

That your place is a time
and that time is past, and passing
further into the drifting mist
like uneven milestones,
the visual whispers of
a silhouette pilgrim,

the echo of the scramble
of tired boots on loose scree,
the order of gravity
bullying with lies of entropy.
In a blind ascent
faith is all,
every foot fall.

Light Sources I

I sit at the very edge of town, and smoke.
Stars whispering above the street light shout,
Now behind me. I sink so I can float
Beneath the shadows, the cosmos to call.
The red candescence from my draw, draws out
The contours of the last garden wall
At my back. Whereas the iridescent
Yellow flickering, as I light the next
Cigar, makes the stars gently disappear.
As do I, in cloudy reminiscence
And a deeper apprehension of the text
Of myself and the celestial spheres.
I duck below the blows of constant fight
To shiver before the warm starlight.

Frozen...

... The sufferers become the scapegoats.
Frozen in the system's lens
and in the winter's cold...

Light Sources II

I duck below the blows of constant fight
Beneath the ever-present burning gaze,
To shiver before the warm starlight.

Our corneas contain competition,
Our lenses tinted with a violent malaise.
I duck below the blows of constant fight,

Prostrate as if in humble contrition
Yet looking up, one can escape this maze
To shiver before the warm starlight,

And amid the frenzied acquisition
In stillness before the ethereal blaze
I duck below the blows of constant fight.

I stoop beneath my prescribed volition,
Relinquish the script planning out my days,
To shiver before the warm starlight.

Letting dew dampen my ignition,
Cooling from the ravaging raging rays,
I duck below the blows of constant fight
To shiver before the warm starlight.

Window Shopping

Each and every story recites
beads of neglect and abuse
threaded with the hair-thin string
of fragile breath.

a twisting of the will,
a burnt hair smell,
a repeated jolting of already-fractured limbs,
a rubbing of the eyes with sand covered fingertips.

The hands that feed
often become fists
that beat, and palms
that smother screams.

If you want to help
you cannot bemoan the teeth.

The papers paint them plastic,
keeping us blind to the cold side
of display windows

where security means
being free from alarms
and able to sleep a night
without the disturbing displacement
of officers of arbitrary enforcement.

Joy in Sunlight

Daybreak was laughing for you.

It was spring for the first time in a decade.

Blue enticed smiles.
Clouds gone from the sky
And into your brain.

An amnesia that blocks sorrow.

Joy in sunlight.

After The Assault

There is hope in the bruises.
But there is no cure,
only the rumour
of prevention
of repetition.

It's quiet
amongst the clattering chaos
of dropped creations.
Broken.

Do not try to gather yourself
into one flawed container.
Try to find new uses
for the displaced fragments of your whole,
that still ring with the sound of their shattering.

It is true,
these fists have changed your future,
but to admit that,
is not to admit defeat.

Blood-Water

There's a dissonance in the rain,
tiny moments of silence interrupted
by repeating aqueous impact,
running into streams;
the capillary veins from the sea-sky heart,
out to the artery clouds.
The earth respires in water
and everything can breathe.

Learning to Move

Scars are the cement of my skin, and I
Dissolve in the thick liquid of her gaze.
I wait for opportunities that rise
And fall, always backing the wrong future.
I collect fool's rocks with a golden glaze
And willfully chase the spaces between dreams.
Scars are the proofs of yesterday's suture
And I dissolve in the grey of endless waiting.
Conflicted, with one foot beyond the seam,
Planted in tomorrow's shifting shadows.
But now I dissolve in truth, sedating
The stubborn ambitions of my ego
I dissolve. I lose my fear of drowning.
I can move. Feel the unknown future's crowning.

Edge

I wanted to look out
from the edge of the world
and feel the weight of
a thousand miles of ocean
breaking against my toes.

I wanted to look out,
to fearlessly stand on
overhanging cliff face,
adding to the nothing before me
with my breath.

I wanted to look out
from the flat of my back
at the immeasurable depth
of the blackness between the stars,
all thinly veiled in our life-parcel atmosphere.

Give me distance:

so I can taste
the untampered air
of the sea;

so I can see
a thousand peaked horizon
reverberating the globe
before my feebly observing eyes;

so I can be
pinned to the earth by starlight,
whose heat and fury
is refracted by light-years
to become peace and beauty.

Give me sea,
give me mountains,
give me stars,
and keep your phony medicine.

Feet

There's something so striking
in caring for other's feet.

Because toes tesselate
by misshaping each other,

pushing and giving way
like office personalities.

Elegant in their uniqueness.
Hidden in their ugliness.
Beautified in the scars or walking.

Convalescence...

*... Yet despite the script
recovery can germinate.*

*Crystalised vapour can proudly exhibit
the humble kintsugi beauty
of anterior struggle.*

Autumn

Autumn returned today,
and it bit my skin.

It didn't make me shiver.
It made angry summer
seethe in my bones.

It caught me unawares
and stranded.

Its grey took my focus from walking
and drove my feet into the road,

searching for the burning core
to offset the indifference of chill.

But I should not be vegetation
and let the climate dictate
my flowering and my fall;

I can choose to retain my leaves
through the frost,

remaining ready to catch
the earliest rays of the thaw.

The Thaw

I am thawing.
I will soon be liquid.
For now I crack
with violent snaps,
And in contrast
I serenely drip, drip,
ripples expanding into
relaxation.

I am thawing.
I will soon be liquid.
For now I exist
in two separate forms.
One: hard, unbending,
cold, unfeeling.
The other: calm,
laughing in movement,
penetrable in stillness.

I am alive in both.

I am thawing,
and I'll soon be useful again. . . .

Absolution

I've seen the scars of your
developing years,
they match the knuckles
of your guardians.

Know this,
you are an innocent perpetrator
of the darkest of sins,

for those were your suckling years.
And as a cub you learned to bite
and as a man you've learned again

and the way the walls hit your fists
is now your solace.

The only escape
is a punishment you cannot live through,
a love your guilt will not let you receive,
a childhood your self-consciousness will not let you re-enter.

The only escape
is a punishment
a love
a childhood.

The only escape
is death and new life.

Made

Yellow teeth have tasted tobacco,
scarred skin has felt the knife,
grey hairs have withstood life:

Fearfully and wonderfully weathered.

Calloused fingers have pressed the strings,
cracked bones have tried utterly,
bruised wrists have broken free:

Fearfully and wonderfully blemished.

Faltering feet know they have strayed,
dejected eyes have been accused,
Yet contrite hearts shall not be refused:

Fearfully and wonderfully stained.

Secure voices can resonate devotion,
crooked limbs have been reset,
repeating lips do not forget:

Fearfully and wonderfully re-made.

Capture Me Now

take me from my daily crises.
they're growing
in the shadows of want.

entice me with sugar
and close the lid tight
inside something that frees

where my wings
can be bound to my shoulders

where they will unfold
from the brittle crust
to bid welcome to new movement

to beat the wind
to cause my feet
to rise from the dust.

Growing

Domestic thoughts
chase shadows up the walls
and stare into corners.

Oh my time away from listening
was always spent shouting
burning words at fire,
wasting my breathe.

Glare a doorway into your wall
and let someone else in
to change your world.
It's not easy.

Slow Freedom

Subtle chains
always linger,

their clinking echoes in the atmosphere
long after the metal has been dissolved.

Every type of freedom is infant at conception
and feeble in its dependance on sacrifice.

Expect to have to nurture your emancipation
as you fight to breathe unpolluted air
with newly purchased lungs.

Home

Home has no concrete definition,
Only further abstract descriptors,
Like belonging, like comfort.
But home is always solid.
Everyone with one
Knows exactly where it is.
Everyone without one
Is drained of strength to stand,
And forbidden to be more
Than searching.

People make a home,
Kisses make a home,
Solitary comfort makes a home,
The right place to be alone,
Contradictions, harmony and
Discord: a home.
Four walls and a roof
Containing sovereignty
The right to be
With or without whatever.
The freedom to be
Naked.
The liberty to be enclosed.
A building blanket in
A cold and exacting wild,
A garden for savage personality
To unfurl uninhibited
By the moulds and maps of
A digitising civilisation.

Human
For Alastair McIntosh.

You are not a building,
Made from moulded bricks
To aesthetic and functional
specifications.

Your shape emerges from
The colliding tectonics beneath the surface,
The wind will texture your skin
Exposing the sedimentary layers
That are yours alone,
Betraying kinship with
Every texture of soil,
Shade of rock
And shape of shards of slate.

No one uses a mountain
But those who want to change its gradient,
Reduce its height,
Plunder the minerals of its dirt flesh.

And no one uses a mountain,
They relate to its height and gradient in
Ascetic ascension and wonder.

After Being Homeless

This is luxury,
this room of white walls
decorated with parts
of my personality.

This is luxury:
this bed,
this duvet,
these pillows,
these walls,

this home.

Response
(to the reader)

Sun fractures days
into peaks and troughs
of past-times.

People lock themselves
in cages made of droplets
and eat themselves
into inefficiency.

Yet there is joy in the downpour
as well as in the blaze,
if you listen for the impact
of water upon dead leaves.

Beyond the meta tricks,
garments will still be soiled in
profoundly juvenile sounds,
like laughter.
And that is no price to pay
for living.

Go! grasp the garden
with both hands
and paint the walls
of your house with earth.